COVER

Douglas Houghton Falls between Laurium and Lake Linden.   Hoyt Avery

Copper Country— God's Country

Copyright 1973
First Edition   May 1973
Second Edition   August 1973
Third Edition   March 1977
by Thomas Avery & Avery Color Studios
AuTrain, Michigan 49806
Library of Congress Card Number 73-76429

Lake Superior shoreline near Eagle River.   Ron Avery

For Dorothy Avery,
who puts up with our unusual hours, moods and miscellaneous idiosyncrasies — And still has it in her to encourage us . . .

FOREWORDS

As a member of a family that traces back four generations living in this mysterious fingerlike tip of real estate, jutting proudly out into Lake Superior, I look with great interest upon the work of the Averys —"Copper Country, God's Country." I have a deep feeling for this land and share a respect for those, who, like the Averys attempt to depict through words and pictures the beauty of the Copper Country.

It is a challenge to undertake a task to explain this Copper Country. Yet, the Averys have done justice to our treasured history and our natural heritage. One can only appreciate their efforts to capture the scenes of the Copper Country, alluding to a country which must "be lived with, endured, admired, but never tamed or greatly altered by the presence of mere man." We who have lived here for so many years tend to view the Copper Country on what was, rather than on what is! We pour through the annals of history expounding on our past greatness to the strangers who trespass our land.

The Averys, now have come into this region, camera in hand, wanting to explore our back roads to discover our present station. For it is on the backroads, in the deserted and ghostlike mining locations, in the rugged emerald tree country, that a visitor can really grasp the beauty of the Copper Country. Yes, they have tred upon our beauty spots, and by use of camera, have captured the true greatness and beauty of this Lake Superior country.

Several years ago, there were those who said the Copper Country had died, but we who have seen death believe more strongly in rebirth as a matter of fact. Last fall as I witnessed a sleek DC-9 swooping down upon an ultra modern jetport located on former farm and mining land — flying over early mining settlements like Houghton and Hancock with their new high rise educational and financial buildings, and expanding residential home sites — my mind turned for a moment to what "was," realizing the importance now of what "is"!

The foundation remains of an abandoned mine shaft in Allouez. Deserted log structures stand at Victoria.

The lonely headstones remain at Eagle River.

A rusting hulk of a railroad plow remains at Quincy.

All attest to the vigor that abounded in the Copper Country.

But, nothing is so consistent as change. The Copper Country is now finding a new place in the sun! It strives to protect its beauty in light of renewed activity which is certain to transform the countryside and quaint little hamlets.

We hear the hue and cry of those who would demolish the old stack at Gay, the crumbling walls at Phoenix, the block houses at Quincy — remains of glory rivaling that of ancient Rome. What is wrong in trying to protect a huge mine hoist at Quincy, in restoring a great opera house in Calumet, in preserving the mining hamlet of Central, in restricting trespassing on the ruins of Mandan? We have both a responsibility to protect and preserve the past especially when it does not hamper progress!

I highly recommend the reading of this work, although it will take a personal tour of the region to fully appreciate the greatness of "Copper Country, God's Country."

William Barkell

WILLIAM BARKELL
Past President
Houghton County Historical Society
Lake Linden, Michigan

Americans know Lake Superior as the "shining Big-Sea-Water" of Longfellow's "Song of Hiawatha," and as a waterway over which the voyageurs drove their canoes on the way into the fur-rich wilderness of Canada.

Beyond that, most have learned little of the story of the northern Great Lakes region.

A major segment of Lake Superior history is the saga of copper: from the obscure, prehistoric metal-gathering of more than 3,000 years ago, to the "copper rush" which took off in the early 1840's, through the development and decline of an industry that wrested billions of pounds of metal from unique and tenacious geological formations.

Thoroughly at home with the traditions and scenic beauties of this land, the Averys use text and color photographs to tell that fascinating story; describing the setting, the mining operations, and the ghosts of the rich and rough mining towns.

The mines today are empty. Deserted are the communities they built. Yet in Lake Superior a bounteous nature has left a rich legacy of pristine beauty and undefiled waters. Safeguarding these treasures for those who come after us is our responsibility and privilege. To me, that message is the soul of this book.

NATHANIEL P. REED,
Assistant Secretary of the Interior
Washington, D.C.

INTRODUCTION

When a writer, particularly a writer-photographer, begins a project dealing with Michigan's renowned Copper Country, he is enthralled with and finally overwhelmed by the tremendous contrast between that world portrayed in numerous volumes of existing type and the one which appears through his camera's viewfinder.

The writer-photographer must attempt to relate the Copper Country saga in a manner which gives the reader clear perspective of what this region is all about, while being able to visually portray only those things which remain to record on film.

It is a difficult assignment.

Each photograph tempers the writer's words and whets his curiosity.

His questions mount as he learns more about what was here once . . . but isn't now. He faces a challenge of pulling two ends of history together without being able to illustrate what has fallen between.

His words, the reader's imagination and the remains of an era must shout of history, character and frontier life, for the echoes of these elements are the lasting part of what happened here. Each reader must keep all this in mind for he will be unable to leave the Copper Country, even from a literary visit, with fewer than a thousand questions to whom there will be no one to ask. It is a fascinating project when today one begins to contemplate the Copper Country story!

Barely 60 years have elapsed since this was among the world's richest copper producing regions. Only 130 years have passed since the first thousands dashed off to brave the remote northern wilderness in search of fabulous riches.

It is indeed ironic that more visible evidence remains to herald the accomplishments of ancient Egyptian Pharaohs than remains of the "modern day" settlers who labored to remove more than 10 billion pounds of red metal from the Copper Countryside! Huge piles of poor rock, crumbling buildings and abandoned railways constitute primary reminders of the colorful days of the copper rush.

Company town and the Quincy shafthouse atop Quincy Hill at Hancock.   Hoyt Avery

So little is left which would indicate that vast fortunes have been made and lost here; that cities and stamping mills and businesses had sprung up and flourished here; that the Copper Country population was larger by 10 times than in these days of population explosion and overcrowded cities.

Today, thousands visit the Copper Country to partake of an undeniably beautiful landscape and the area's much publicized "pure and vitalizing air," but few modern travelers think about the days when more roadway was being maintained beneath this country than winds across it today. One must continually remind himself that this scenic region became famous for copper mining!

The quiet countryside was disturbed for a brief moment in history and quickly resettled itself to be enjoyed by sightseers, rockhounds and amateur historians. The face of the landscape was rearranged, but not in a manner which leaves the scars remaining on many of the world's mining districts. The Copper Country just took on additional character and went about covering the evidence of man's encroachment with trees and natural reclamation projects.

The Copper Country is certainly rich in history — to the point that many who helped make it are still living. But most of the trappings which would reflect such a rich and colorful past lie scattered in various stages of decay, victims of hard times and a losing battle with the relentless elements of this rugged environment.

It's a simple fact of Copper Country life that much of what happened here is lost but for fading memories of old-timers and records on stacks of yellowed paper. A writer must attempt much "between the lines" research as fond memories and reports, written in the heat of the times, tend to be somewhat romanticized. And still the overstated memories and exaggerated reports are nearly all that remain of so many communities like Mandan, Gay, Central, Phoenix, Clifton, Fort Wilkins, Rockland, Lake Linden, Silver City, Victoria, Mass — dozens of places where scattered foundations and rock piles offer testimony to the flourishing activity once taken for granted here.

The people who live here today, largely descendants of the world's mining nationalities, accepted the decline of the copper industry with the stern faced resolve common to miners everywhere.

Many have remained at other jobs in the district, awaiting the discovery or accident of economic history which would make it profitable to begin mining again. Many more moved to other mining districts around the United States or to industrial centers where work was plentiful.

The now famous White Pine Mining Company, which began operations near the western reaches of the Copper Country, created jobs for many who continued to believe in the future of this copper lined region. The boom days are probably gone forever, but White Pine keeps the Copper Country story alive and it continues — from Isle Royale to White Pine, from 3000 B.C. to the 20th Century. Here is a tale that becomes more interesting each day. . . .

The words and pictures in this volume are directed at piquing interest, at increasing historical awareness and most importantly, at telling the Copper Country story from its beginnings in post glacial prehistory to the present.

I hope that some of these objectives will be realized and that every page will inspire at least one more person to seek out the fascinating lore and beauty of Michigan's Copper Country.

Rapids on the Sturgeon River, near Sturgeon River Canyon and Falls north of Sidnaw.   Hoyt Avery

were bested only by those of Isle Philippeaux to the south and the gem crusted Keweenaw Peninsula jutting into the icy lake.

Franklin, certainly aware of the importance of metallic resources in building a new nation and supposedly overwhelmed by the evidence placed before him, negotiated a treaty which would insure American possession of any riches which might indeed lie in the Superior countryside.

The first formal recognition of the Copper Country came with the drawing of a line on a crude map of the New World and the Great Lakes region. It would be a long time before the area again enjoyed such international notoriety.

The new international boundary extended, approximately as today, from New England up the St. Lawrence River and through the centers of Lakes Ontario, Erie and Huron until it entered Lake Superior. Here it stabbed out in a northwesterly direction, taking in Isle Royale and Isle Philippeaux, before dropping sharply again to the southwest and back to the center of the lake.[5]

As the treaty ink dried, early explorers were heading off to fill homespun pockets with the gold, silver, rubies and gems of the "Copper Country."

At the same time, Patrick Henry stood before Congress, pointing out the failure of English adventurer Alexander Henry who had opened and abandoned the first unsuccessful Superior mining attempt in 1770-71. The English were only too glad to be rid of this "fag end of creation" which Henry said was better left to the animals and savages who roamed the dense forest.

Patrick Henry concluded his address to Congress with an apt description of the Superior countryside ... "The entire region is beyond the most distant wilderness and remote as the moon."

Memories of Franklin's persistent bargaining at the peace table and the reasoning behind the strange boundary line in Lake Superior grew dimmer. Pressure was often applied in efforts to speed exploration of the area, but Congress simply approved the proposals and then ignored moves to follow through with any such projects. The Nation and Congress turned to more important undertakings. . . .

Very little interest generated from possession of the Michigan wilderness during the 60 years following the Revolution.

Although 1,000 trappers and traders passed through the Straits each year on their way to and from the rich peltlands of the unexplored Upper Peninsula, no permanent settlements were established away from the Detroit and Mackinac areas.

That the British were allowed to maintain garrisons at both places for more than 15 years after war's end is indicative of the new nation's lukewarm interest in the Upper Lakes region. Even more importantly, this illustrated the United States' inability to supply men or resources with which to protect the 500 pioneer settlers encamped there. It was consensus that if the British were willing to assume the burden of protecting the area from the Indian menace, there was little urgency in demanding their withdrawal.

Anthony Wayne's defeat of the Indians in the Northwest Territory and ratification of the Constitution endowed Congress with authority to create treaties and to negotiate land purchases with the Indians. Wayne's victory eased the situation and British withdrawal was at last demanded in 1796.

Plans were laid for construction of a Federal Union, through the territorial settlement and development plan of the Northwest Ordinance and a new burst of westward expansion occurred as pioneers began purchasing government lands in the new territories at a cash price of $1.25 an acre.

Prior claims to Michigan were relinquished by Pennsylvania, Massachusetts and Virginia as the Northwest Territory was created, complete with survey plans and the provisions for territorial statehood.[6]

From 1796 to 1800, the Michigan area was administered as part of the Northwest Territory. In 1800, the area was divided between the Northwest and the newly formed Indiana Territory. The Great Lake State remained divided until the Indiana Territory was enlarged to include the entire region in 1803.

The Michigan Territory, finally established by Congress in 1805, included the entire Lower Peninsula and the extreme eastern portion of the Upper. The western Upper Peninsula, including the Copper Country, remained part of the huge Indiana Territory. No one seemed especially concerned over possession of the Upper Lakes region and the entire area remained only partially explored and almost entirely ignored as development continued elsewhere.

Fur traders continued to wander throughout the area, their efforts reaping huge profits for John Jacob Astor and his American Fur Company. French and British companies also continued trapping operations throughout the wilderness. Boatloads of furs moved around the Great Lakes as various companies prospered in absence of government jurisdiction. Profits went everywhere but to the Indians who harvested the pelts.

Few written accounts (aside from financial ledgers), were maintained by the hardy traders and frontiersmen who first explored the virgin forests, but the stories they passed along hinted of things to come in Michigan's Copper Country.

Their homespun yarns of exploration and discovery began to weave increasing credibility into the fabric of those exaggerated tales which had first stirred interest in the area. Mention of gold, silver and precious gems was not entirely absent from their stories, but copper was becoming the more common central topic.

Existence of huge copper masses or boulders was verified, while the traders' dealings with local Indians added continually to the skimpy knowledge of the Copper region. Many Indians possessed specimens of copper recovered from Lake Superior beaches or passed down from former generations. They treasured these as Manitous, messages promising good fortune from the gods of the Lake Superior tribes. There is little mention of copper tools or weapons in the possession of the Indians, although they spoke of mysterious mines where strange and dangerous vapors were given off and the metal could be obtained. The copper they possessed was probably free float copper torn loose from larger deposits.

Fresh beaver cuttings near Chippewa Harbor Trail, Isle Royale National Park.   Tom Avery

In any case, they willingly showed white traders where surface specimens might be acquired and apparently placed little value upon the metal as they made no attempt to conceal its presence.[7]

Strange tales of extensive ancient mines, mentioned by earlier explorers and missionaries, were also carried to civilization by the trappers. They said that the Indians knew of these mines from the ancient hammerstones which lie scattered throughout the region.[8]

The Indians did not know who had worked these diggings, how or why they had extracted the copper, or how long ago they had vanished from the area. These intriguing stories and others began to rekindle flagging interest in the country's mineral resources.

As the remainder of the nation was busily engaged in the business of settlement, growth and expansion, these rugged woodsmen were adding to the stockpile of "handy things to know about the Michigan Copper Country." They also opened the door on one of those fascinating historical puzzles which leaves archeologists, scientists and engineers scratching their collective heads . . . each theorizing as to what might have been.

I refer to the extensive prehistoric mining operations once carried on from Isle Royale, along the Keweenaw Peninsula and throughout the entire copper producing region some 3,500 to 4,000 years ago.[9]

These miners left no burial grounds, dwellings, pottery, clay tablets or cave drawings. The mystery of their origin remains unsolved. Little cultural evidence was left behind to tell where these people had come from — only thousands of copper producing pits and more thousands of crude hammering stones with which the pits had been worked.

The ancients apparently worked the copper bearing rock by alternately applying fire and cold water, thus breaking the rock into smaller pieces from which they could extract the metal with hand held hammering stones or stone hatchets.[10]

Professor Roy Drier and Octave DuTemple have compiled and published a fascinating study of *Prehistoric Copper Mining In The Lake Superior Region*, in which many diversified theories are expressed regarding origins and mining methods of the ancients.

DuTemple points out in the introduction that the mines were probably worked only during the warmer months as there is no indication of permanent settlement. Assuming that the work was seasonal, scientists and engineers estimate that it would have required 10,000 men 1,000 years to develop the extensive operations carried on throughout the region!

DuTemple's scientific approach sneaks up on every reader and then staggers even the most vivid imagination.

He relates, "If one assumes that an average pit is 20 feet in diameter and 30 feet deep, then it appears that something like 1,000 to 1,200 tons of ore were removed per pit. If the ore averaged 5 per cent, or 100 pounds per ton then approximately 100,000 pounds of copper were removed per pit. If 5,000 pits existed, as earlier estimates indicated (and all pits are copper producing), then 100,000 pounds per pit in 5,000 pits means that 500,000,000 pounds of copper were mined in prehistoric times — all of it without anything more than fire, stone hammers and manpower. If the ore sampled 15 per cent, and if more than 5,000 pits existed, then over 1.5 billion pounds of copper were mined."[11]

Lake Superior shoreline near Copper Harbor.
Ron Avery

The Lake of the Clouds, Porcupine Mountains State Park.
Hoyt Avery

Additional observations make this Copper Country riddle even more perplexing —

For one thing, Lake Superior copper was, until recently, the world's only known source of native copper.[12] That copper tools and ornaments were reported without exeception by every New World explorer, (Columbus in Yucatan, Cortez in Mexico, and Cartier, Raleigh and DeSoto among others in the Southern and Atlantic United States), is indicative of the sophisticated prehistoric trading network which moved Lake Superior copper to every part of North and South America.

Where the bulk of prehistoric copper production went, or was intended to go, remains a mystery along with the reason for abandoning the mines. Whatever the answers, the open pits had filled with soil and were supporting a second or third generation of 200 year old forest when Columbus "discovered" the riches of the New World in the 15th Century!

Archeologists concur that abandonment of Superior mining operations had not been anticipated by the ancients. The tools with which they worked were left as though work were to resume the following morning. For some unknown reason the work never resumed. The ancients gathered their belongings and left the mined copper where it lay separated from rock at the edges of the pits. It would be found just as they left it by 17th Century explorers.

Theories concerning the origin of this metallurgically cultured society continue to spring forth. Every discovery — a previously unknown ocean current, completion of another Thor Heyrdahl expedition, the finding of Lake Superior copper at the site of some far distant early culture, brings forth a new wave of scientific theory. And, as time even changes geography, it is likely that the Copper Country will persist in keeping her heretofore well-guarded secret.

Prehistoric mining display at Fort Wilkins State Park. Note the grooved hammering stones, found only at the prehistoric pits on the Keweenaw Peninsula. The stones discovered on Isle Royale were ungrooved and are believed to have been brought there from the Thunder Bay, Ontario region. Tom Avery

Looking northwest toward Ontario and the Sleeping Giant from atop the Minong Ridge, Isle Royale National Park. Both prehistoric and modern mining operations were carried out near this location.   Ron Avery

Bete Grise Bay near Smith Fisheries.　　　　Hoyt Avery

*Sunrise over Copper Harbor and Lake Fanny Hooe
from Brockway Mountain Drive.*　　　　Hoyt Avery

Stories of riches continued to trickle southward as the new nation became more populous. The 1820 census enumerated 8,765 persons in the Michigan Territory. The number reached 31,640 by 1830 and then tripled in the next four years. A Territorial Census counted 87,278 in 1834 — 85,856 living in the Lower Peninsula.[13]

The Erie Canal had opened and an influx of farmers began spilling into Michigan. Thousands came seeking richer and more abundant lands than they could obtain in crowded New York, Massachusetts and other marginally productive Northeastern States. Business of every sort followed in their wake.

Three tiers of southern counties were quickly settled and were governing themselves when the Territory applied for admission to the Union in 1833.

A constitution was drafted in 1835. It was submitted for voter approval one day, followed by election of territorial-state officials the next.

The electorate overwhelmingly approved the constitution and subsequently named Stevens T. Mason as Territorial Governor and then two years were to pass before Michigan entered the Federal Union with an Upper Peninsula consolation prize dumped squarely in its young lap.

A boundary dispute had arisen over ownership of a narrow strip of land extending along Michigan's southern border. It was eventual settlement of this southernmost boundary which led to establishment of the State's northernmost. Had the results been different, exploration and development of the Copper Country would likely have been postponed for at least 50 years.

In a nutshell, Ohio, which became a state in 1803, and Michigan both claimed the area surrounding Toledo, where the Maumee River entered Lake Erie. As several major canal networks would converge at this point, each sought to exercise its respective claims to the area.

Both "states" had surveys (bought and paid for by interested citizens), and reams of legal documentation to substantiate their ownership rights.

Michigan finally resorted to dispatching the "state" militia to enforce her claims. Ohio officials, however, entered the disputed area at night, convened in legal sessions and dispersed by daylight, thus maintaining legal jurisdiction by right of a governing body acting within the Ohio Strip. . . .

And so the "Ohio War" was fought.

The issue was a complicated one, the opponents serious in their claims to jurisdiction, and the resultant "war" about as monumental as Halloween!

Both sides "trick or treated" back and forth across the area. No one was killed or wounded although black eyes and broken knuckles were not uncommon in proximity of the Maumee River. Meanwhile, the entire matter was conveniently neglected by the President and Congress as they awaited 1836 elections.

Andrew Jackson, the master of practical politics, had no desire to anger large numbers of Ohio, Indiana or Illinois voters as he toiled to assure protege Martin Van Buren's election over William Henry Harrison of Ohio. Jackson accordingly removed upstart Stevens T. Mason from the Michigan Territorial Governor's Office and urged Congress to settle the issue "favorably" before the 1836 election.

Right may have been on one side as surveys and the Northwest Ordinance indicate, but political power was overwhelmingly on the side of Ohio.

Middle Branch of the Ontonagon River near Agate Falls.
Hoyt Avery

Five Mile Point west of Eagle River.   Ron Avery

In June, 1836, Jackson signed the compromise-ultimatum which said that Michigan would be admitted as a state "if" its people would accept the boundary compromise. The proposal would give Ohio the Maumee River area in question, but Michigan would receive the vast Upper Peninsula and all the potential riches that went with it.

Needless to say, sentiment against the compromise was nearly universal.

A Territorial Resolution adopted in March, 1836, renounced the Upper Peninsula consolation prize as a "sterile region on the shores of Lake Superior, destined by soil and climate to remain forever a wilderness."

Nevertheless, a hastily called and questionably legal Territorial Convention met in Detroit, where it approved the compromise in an 11th hour December decision. . . . Michigan received title to the western three quarters of the Upper Peninsula in exchange for relinquishment of all claims to the Ohio Strip.

A month later Michigan became the 26th state in the Federal Union and the way was clear for the beginning of the copper rush in what had finally become the Upper Peninsula of Michigan.

Early winter on Lake Superior near Copper Harbor.
Ron Avery

In 1820, Territorial Governor Lewis Cass and explorer-geologist Henry Schoolcraft had skirted the shoreline area of the Upper Peninsula. Leaving Mackinac Island, Cass and his 65-man party moved slowly along Superior's southern coast. They proceeded to the mouth of the Ontonagon River and Schoolcraft ascended the river to view the famed copper boulder reported by numerous early travelers.[14]

At this point, the party was divided and exploration continued throughout the Territory. Despite this first well-chronicled effort and Schoolcraft's later work near the Soo, little more than superficial light was shed on the nature or extent of the vast land area which had suddenly become part of Michigan in 1837.

Most Michiganders, still redfaced at the results of the Ohio Compromise, viewed the Upper Peninsula as the State's single greatest "sorrow." They were certainly less than excited by the offer of a young Detroit physician, Douglas Houghton, to go off and explore it.[15]

Remains of Minong Ridge mining operations, Isle Royale National Park.   Ron Avery

Wilderness trail, Isle Royale National Park.

Tom Avery

Stevens T. Mason, Michigan's first elected Governor, and a personal friend of Houghton's, established the office of State Geologist, appointed Houghton and somehow managed to persuade a reluctant legislature of farmers and shop keepers to allocate $3,000 to finance the first year of exploration.

Houghton, only 29 when he offered his service to Mason, had already made several trips to the Superior region and felt there must be some fact in the copper plated rumors which had persisted for centuries. His careful scientific approach made him acceptable for the assignment even though he was not a geologist. That he probably knew as much as any person alive about the Upper Peninsula wilderness was another key factor in his selection.

He had accompanied Schoolcraft on expeditions in 1831 and 1832, had also visited and hacked off a piece of the Ontonagon boulder and had long dreamed of an extensive search for the area's copper treasures. Limited time and financial backing and the general lack of interest in the region had thus far thwarted him, but in 1840 Houghton was at last able to set out with the resources needed to find out what was really up there.

The $3,000 doled out by a conservative state government was certainly the

Eagle Harbor Lighthouse, manned and operated by U.S. Coast Guard at Eagle Harbor.   Hoyt Avery

most financially rewarding piece of Michigan legislation ever enacted.[16]

Through the summer and fall of 1840, Houghton and a small group of assistants systematically explored the Copper Country wilderness, returning to Detroit only when winter threatened to leave them stranded.

The party had indeed located copper along Lake Superior and evidence that it had been deposited in commercial quantities. But Houghton was careful to mark every statement regarding the area with scientific reservation and caution. It is no wonder that so little excitement accompanied news of his findings and return to Detroit!

Houghton spent weeks preparing his report for the State Legislature. When he finally stood before its members in December, his summary was a characteristic model of calculated understatement.

The interest he sparked by reports of "rich and abundant ores of copper" was doused in the same sentence when he warned that "skill, money and organization were necessary before fortunes could be taken from the south shore of Lake Superior."

Excitement fizzled and evaporated as congressmen realized the impossibility of organizing the huge amounts of capital needed to promote mining activities in the middle of nowhere. It was certainly not an area for individual endeavor and no Michigan businessman or legislator was anxious to lay a personal fortune on the line in pursuit of such a risky, foolhardy venture—

But offer a prospect of riches and the foolhardy will materialize from somewhere to seek them out and if Houghton's report stirred little enthusiasm in the halls of legislature, the opposite was true in the cities, factories and on the farms to the south and east. From his lengthy and calculated report to the State Legislature only a few passages were recalled—

"With a single blast I threw out nearly two tons of ore. With this there were many masses of native copper from the most minute specks to one of about 40 pounds in weight."

Charles Penny, who accompanied the Houghton expedition, relates in his diary, that on July 7, 1840, the party threw nearly five tons of rock from a vein near the entrance to Copperas Harbor.[17]

Penny writes, "About one-fifth was good ore, worth 50 per cent. The other four tons contained more or less copper. . . . Still he (Dr. Houghton), thinks the veins discovered a few miles east of the Little Montreal or Cascade River will prove more valuable."

Houghton's warnings, all the ifs, ands, and buts, were soon lost amid talk of the solid copper mountains of Keweenaw. Even unpuffed statements such as Penny's were construed as promises of wealth.

A few would-be copper barons came to Keweenaw in 1841.

Another handful traveled to the area in 1842. That year the Chippewa ceded all claims to 30,000 square miles of Upper Peninsula real estate to the United States Government.

The last hurdle to Copper Country exploration, the removal of the Indian menace, had been cleared with expenditure of little more than government-financed tobacco for the peace pipe.

The big copper rush was on before the ice left Lake Superior in spring, 1843. Douglas Houghton's warnings were all but forgotten in the days to come, as hundreds, then thousands dashed off to the Upper Peninsula. This was the beginning of that insane era in American history when almost everyone wanted to get in on one of the rushes to riches.

Many of the famous 49'ers would cut their teeth on Keweenaw copper.

The folk heroes of future generations would be born here among the ramshackle buildings of America's first mining boom towns.

The characters: miners, saloon keepers, madams, whiskey drummers, claim jumpers, brawlers, millionaires, paupers — would be immortalized in every mining camp still to come. These were the people whose exploits would fill the pages of the dime novel, the comic book and would someday be the center of attention on televisions in nearly every American living room.

The places would change — from Sutter's Mill to the Black Hills to the Klondike. . . .

The treasures would change — from copper to gold to silver to land. . . .

But the stories, names, faces and plots would remain the same. Here were the beginnings of a madcap era in American history, a continual case of cultural shock and counter shock — and it all really began happening for the first time in Keweenaw!

Only a few more facts are needed to attain true perspective of what was starting to develop here. They make the story of the copper boom in the Upper Peninsula seem even more incredible.

For one thing, these first prospectors (if one can conscientiously dub them such), were risking everything to seek out riches in copper, a base metal valued at cents-per-pound rather than dollars-per-ounce. It would require literally tons of copper to create anything which might remotely resemble a fortune!

Secondly, the thousands who rushed off to Copper Country knew almost nothing of geology, mining, potential markets or how to transport their findings if they indeed got lucky. The only form in which many had ever seen copper was as a tea kettle or a highly polished boiler resting beside the kitchen range!

As one becomes more familiar with the Copper Country and the south shore of Lake Superior, it becomes even more impossible to believe that people would actually rush off to such an area, trusting as they must have, that everything would take care of itself — But they did and it did!

There were no roads in the area. Everything came and went by ship on an unpredictable Lake Superior.

In winter only a dog team could travel. Starvation and death from exposure were always a threat. Loss of a provision ship, especially a late season deliverer of winter food stuffs, meant certain disaster. This was especially true when one considers mining attempts on Isle Royale and equally isolated areas of the impenetrable mainland.

The entire frenzied affair rang of mass insanity and yet somehow worked itself out through sheer inertia and a sizeable dose of blind luck!

How the individual miner ever hoped to prosper is an impossible question, but some did get rich, their successes spurring the organization of the vast financial resources and mining companies which would carry the Copper Country dream to fruition.

Remains of the Allouez Mine No. 4 at Ahmeek on the Keweenaw Peninsula.   Hoyt Avery

Copper Harbor Lighthouse. It was on this point that Douglas Houghton did some prospecting and where the Pittsburgh and Boston Mining Company began mining in the first days of the copper boom.   Ron Avery

It is hard for 20th Century man to visualize these first mining efforts. Our familiarity with technology makes it easier to imagine how difficult mining must have been. It becomes easier to imagine what early miners had to work with than what they lacked!

We are all familiar with dozens of everyday uses for copper. Try listing them and then remember that we are considering a copper mining boom which began in the middle 1840's.

Electricity was still a misunderstood element of thunderstorms. There was only man and animal power with which to dig, move tons of rock and haul away the copper to wherever it had to go for shipment. There were no electric lights or ventilation systems either above or below ground. And there was no market for the millions of miles of copper wiring which today carry electricity into nearly every home.

Fort Wilkins State Park near Copper Harbor. Built to protect prospectors from the threat of Indian attack and manned until 1870, this historic location has been restored and is open to the public.   Hoyt Avery

The telegraph employed copper wire and had been in use for about six years when mining began in the Upper Peninsula, but the telephone and electric light would not come until 1876 and 1879, respectively. This means nearly 25 years of mining before creation of electric power — an important tool in today's mines and a major market for the finished product. . . .

Even the AC motor, diesel and gasoline engines were far in the future. Each contributed much to later mining efficiency and again created huge new markets for copper.

History tends to jumble together for most of us. We can't realize how long ago 1843 really was until it's aligned with other events we recall as ancient history!

A few examples —

The famed Pony Express was 15 years in the future.

Dynamite, which we automatically associate with mining, wouldn't be invented until 1862!

And Custer would not make his last stand at the Little Big Horn until 1876. . . .

A lot of frontier history certainly remained to be written when the copper rush began in 1843. It seems strange that so much of this area's role in history has been overlooked. . . .

These were the Dark Ages by today's mining, industrial and living standards, yet the crude approach to mining of Lake Superior copper played an important

The military kitchen area, adjacent to the mess hall at Fort Wilkins State Park. Tom Avery

part in creating the technological conveniences, indeed necessities of modern life—

The very discovery and subsequent development of this country's first abundant supply of copper added momentum to industrial and technological advances already occurring at breakneck speed. The primary uses with which we now associate copper didn't exist in 1843, but its discovery again shot the nation down the path to their development and everyday use. . . .

It would be unfair to leave the reader puzzling as to what copper was used for in 1843—

Well, copper made fine cooking utensils. It could be coined or alloyed to make brass and bronze, both important to industry in the times before a plentiful supply of fine steel and iron. Copper was very important in creating corrosion and barnacle resistant hardware and hull covers for our growing navy and merchant marine. It was an integral part of the arms manufacturing industry; cannon, shell casings, and other paraphernalia necessary for waging battle required large amounts of copper.

Copper was a highly valued building material. The green domes and flashings on many Copper Country buildings attest to its permanence.

Still, its uses and the market for the raw metal were certainly limited by today's standards!

So, equipped with historical perspective, let's delve into the acquisition of Superior copper as we explore a few of those famous mining towns mentioned in the introduction. . . .

The rush of copper hunters came clamoring ashore at picturesque Copper Harbor, Ontonagon and Eagle Harbor. Boom towns sprang up everywhere a ship could safely find shelter from Lake Superior.

Few of the would-be copper magnates had the slightest idea of where or how to go about their search for copper. They just kept coming, heading off into the trackless forest and temporarily vanishing while others came ashore and followed suit.

Every day would bring an excited prospector out of the woods with a piece of native metal and the discovery story of another fabulous lode . . . vein . . . or something!

Prospectors were everywhere. They blasted every cliff looking for copper. They spit on rocks to ascertain its presence. They dug holes and sank shafts in search of it. They dug out every depression where ancient miners might have found it. They bored into sheer cliff faces for it — And damned if almost all of them didn't find some copper! Not much generally, but enough to ward off total discouragement and make the swamps, woods, swarms of black flies and mosquitos bearable for a little while longer. These were certainly the predecessors of today's die-hard fishermen!

Anyway, by 1846, the copper rush had begun to run full speed astern as one dream after another pinched out, became barren and died at the bottom of a thousand Copper Country shafts.

An almost total ignorance of the area's geology was a major factor. Nearly all the copper taken prior to 1846 had been float copper, torn loose from larger main deposits and dumped elsewhere by glacial movement thousands of years earlier.

Many times the copper was found in veins created by volcanic action millions of years ago. The copper had found its way into underground holes or fissures,

The remains of Clifton, near the site of the famous Cliff Mine, America's first great mass copper mine.

Tom Avery

Summer stream running past ruins near the Cliff Mine.
Norton Avery

Headstone of a Cornish miner buried in the Eagle River Cemetery.   Hoyt Avery

often miles from any main ore body. Here it waited to trick and discourage early miners.

Bypassing any complicated geological explanations, suffice it to say that most of these fissures were an afterthought of nature. They simply formed convenient receptacles where copper accumulated when there was nowhere else left for it to flow.

The veins discovered by early miners invariably ran at right angles to the real mineral belt of the Copper Country and usually petered out after producing extremely promising amounts of native metal in the first days or weeks of mining. The miners were very simply working in the wrong directions, taking the "overflow" copper from fissures where it had met least resistance and settled ages ago. One can imagine the exasperation that left miners scratching their heads and cursing the country in befuddled confusion.

It is interesting that early prospectors totally ignored the rich amygdaloid copper regions where huge amounts of metal were imbedded in what would later prove to be rich ore rock. This amygdaloid was shot through with copper which had formed in tiny almond-shaped pockets. This ore was deemed worthless until the Isle Royale Mining Company began producing profitable quantities of metal by running their "poor rock" through a relatively primitive stamping mill in 1852.[18] This type of mining would one day prove itself the salvation of the Copper Country.

Another very important point to recognize is that Douglas Houghton's earlier warnings were beginning to manifest themselves with a vengeance by 1846! It would require sizeable amounts of land, labor and capital to create a fortune in the Copper Country. This fact had been largely ignored in the first years of the copper rush.

By 1846, only the Pittsburgh and Boston and the Lake Superior Mining Companies were still operating in the Copper Country. Much early speculation met with disaster. Of the 24 companies formed between 1844 and 1850, only six would pay any dividends and all were organized to mine mass and float copper deposits.[19]

The experience of the Pittsburgh and Boston Company demonstrates why individual efforts could not succeed. For example, in 1844-45, Pittsburgh and Boston stockholders spent $28,000 on diggings near Copper Harbor, realizing but $2,968 from sales of copper. Their experiences on the Copper Harbor Lighthouse Point and near today's concession at Ft. Wilkins were not unique. The Fort Wilkins shaft bottomed at 120 feet and stockholders dug deeper into their pockets so the search might continue elsewhere.

A well maintained and educational attraction remains at Fort Wilkins, constructed in 1844 to protect prospectors from Indian aggression. Although the fort seems to have better served the Indians in any protective capacity, the old stockade on Lake Fanny Hooe near Copper Harbor, was garrisoned on and off until 1870 when it was finally abandoned.

Completely restored, Ft. Wilkins remains as a Michigan State Park where visitors can attain a realistic footing from which to view the history of the Copper Country and the life of the times.

Referring again to mining operations, it is interesting to note that the majority of capital funding came from outstate financiers. The best families of Boston and Pittsburgh were the first to risk their fortunes on Michigan copper ventures.[20]

The silence of winter descends on the Misery Bay area.
Hoyt Avery

Returning to the 1846 exodus from Copper Country, we come to a major turning point in the annals of mining and the Superior copper region.

A profitable mass copper mine was being developed from a fissure vein along a line of sheer cliffs near Eagle River on the Keweenaw Peninsula.

Shortly thereafter the fabulous Cliff Mine began producing the first mass copper that was not also float copper.[21] Huge pieces of metal, some weighing more than 50 tons, were discovered where they had been deposited. They lay deep beneath the surface, undisturbed by the glaciers which had gouged out so many other specimens, scattered them around the country and tricked so many early miners.

Miners did an about face at many Copper Country docks and returned to the hunt or to find work at the Cliff location. In July, 1846, the Cliff's two short shafts produced 510,000 pounds of copper. In August, 350,000 pounds came to the surface. Up to this time, backers of Pittsburgh and Boston had a stock investment of $150,000 and the company had spent $66,128 to produce $8,870 in copper.[22]

This is again indicative of the huge capital reserves necessary to persue Lake Superior copper, but the Cliff would prove out as the region's first bonanza and would repay her backers handsomely in the years ahead.

But even people who had money in the Cliff had moments of doubt before this copper ship came in. The figures for 1846-47, (above), were presented to Pittsburgh and Boston directors along with a stockholder assessment of another $110,000 for continued work on the Cliff diggings. Boston stockholders panicked! They refused to pay and Dr. Charles Avery, chairman of the board and one-fifth owner of the company, was forced to step forward and put his entire fortune, some $80,000, on the line to back continued mining.

The Cliff, at 700 feet, was far and away the deepest of Copper Country mines and stockholders feared another dismal failure. Avery had learned from Cornish miners that European copper mines often did not pay until depths of 800 feet or more had been reached. He was certain that there was more copper buried at Clifton. The only way to find it was to dig until the deposit reappeared and could be exploited.

A year-and-a-half-later, 1849, the Cliff forces again hit rich vein rock. Avery was repaid, paid a bonus equal to his investment and the first dividend payment was made to stockholders in a Copper Country mine.

Financial problems behind, the miners turned to the awesome task of removing mass copper from deep below the surface. Pure copper masses, some weighing 100 tons, were chiselled, hammered, blasted, cut in pieces and hauled to the surface bit by bit.

Smaller pieces of mass copper were packed in barrels for shipping while larger masses were cut only small enough to remove from the mine and were shipped as nearly whole as possible. One can imagine the dock at Copper Harbor covered with huge masses of native copper, mined during the winter and stored there until the spring thaw!

Pieces of rock containing mass copper were gathered separately. If the copper could not be easily extracted for barrel shipment, the rocks would be collectively fired in huge cordwood infernos. Water was poured on the pile at intervals, breaking the heated rocks and laborers could gather the copper when the rock cooled.

The procedure was similar at all Copper Country mass mines. Large forces of surface labor were required to handle the copper once it was removed from the mine. This accounted for the development of self-sufficient little mining communities near the entrance of every mass mining operation.

Each had its own blacksmiths, teamsters, woodsmen, miners and laborers. Work was constantly going on above and below ground. The huge copper pyres mentioned above were burning in continual rotation. Woodsmen toiled to supply timber for shaft and building construction. Teamsters struggled to deliver the copper masses to shipment points. Each community was a complete entity dedicated to only one task, removing copper from the bowels of the countryside.

It is difficult to envision these industrious communities from what remains of Clifton and other mass mine sites such as Copper Falls, Phoenix, Central or Rockland. Massive piles of rock are about all that's left.

For a time all attention was devoted to development of other mass mines. The Minesota Mine, sunk on prehistoric diggings at Rockland, near the Ontonagon River, was paying dividends by 1852. Mass mines at Central, Copper Falls and Phoenix also began producing substantial quantities of copper during the next few years.

The rock in the successful mass mines was so rich that it yielded fine profits, but concentrations of ore proved to be scattered through great areas of poor rock. In all, the mass mines of the Copper Country paid slightly less than $7 million in dividends.[23] Altogether, attempts at mass mining lost many times that amount. Still it was the rich pockets of "easily found" copper in these ore

A small lake near the site of the Minesota Mine at Rockland. Hoyt Avery

bodies which were responsible for the development of the Copper Country.

Had the mass mines been the only ones in the Lake Superior area, the Keweenaw Peninsula would have remained a wilderness dotted with short-lived mining camp ghost towns. If, on the other hand, the mining methods and ore bodies developed during the next 50 years had come first, the history of the Copper Country would have been much shorter. The fortunes would have been made, the reserves depleted and efforts abandoned at a much earlier date than was actually the case.

The mass mines were also important as excellent teachers. The lessons learned in their depths prepared the Nation and the men of the mining district for the glorious future still ahead. These first mines served as splendid labora-tories where geology and mining technology could be worked out with the relatively meager tools of the time.

And one more point which bears repeating — The major uses with which we now associate copper didn't exist in the 1850's. Michigan's mass mines produced all the copper the country could use in the decade before the beginning of the industrial age!

The Cliff's production literally dwarfed the copper output of any previous American mine, but for all intents, the Cliff would be a dead mine only 20 years later. By 1870, the Cliff had returned $2,327,000 to investors, but the seemingly inexhaustable storehouse of copper had been drained. This would happen at all of the region's mass mines as efforts to find additional storehouses of mass copper failed.

Yet, while the mass mines were still in their heyday, discoveries were being made which would eventually compile another important segment of the

The Quincy shafthouse as it appears today. Shafts near this location descend more than 9,000 feet to the Pewabic Amygdaloid lode from which the Quincy produced copper for more than 50 years, earning the title of "Old Reliable."
Tom Avery

Railroad snowplow used for opening the tracks remains
near the Quincy shafthouse.   Hoyt Avery

copper story. To understand this chapter in Copper Country history it is necessary to again reflect briefly on the geology of the copper producing region.

To begin, the copper range was gestated some 800 million years ago. During the next 250 to 300 million years, periodic volcanic disturbances spewed white-hot liquid rock to the surface. The eruptions occurred one after another, each creating a new layer which flowed over and cooled atop the previous ones.

Visualizing a cut-away drawing of the area, the layers would look like a stack of gigantic saucers, flat at the center and curved up at the edges.[24] The flat portion of the stack holds Lake Superior. One bent up edge forms the Lake's north shore. The layers of the other edge comprise the mineral range.

While the successive volcanos were heaving up molten lava, they were also spewing out super-heated volcanic gases. These gases bubbled up through the molten rock. As the lava cooled and hardened, these gas "bubbles" were trapped, creating irregular underground cavities ranging in size from pinhead to amphitheater.

The amygdaloid deposits were formed at this time. Geologists disagree as to what happened next or where Michigan copper came from. The important fact is that these billions of pockets were somehow filled with remarkably pure copper. When they had filled, there was nothing for the remaining copper to do but spill out over the surrounding countryside and proceed along the path of least resistance.

It was this sort of spillover which had been so successfully tapped at Clifton, Rockland, Central and Copper Falls. At a few points such as these, the copper had been deposited in the amphitheater-sized gas pockets just mentioned, but amounts were generally smaller and locations unpredictable. These two factors

Remains of wooden ore cars near Quincy shafthouse.

Ron Avery

account for the failure of the many promising finds which, more often than not, pinched out so suddenly . . . so unexpectedly . . . so dismally. . . .

By 1851, prospectors had discovered copper around the edges of amygdaloid (almond shaped), cavities in the porous rock of the mineral belt. The lava bed or amygdaloid lodes were explored at this time, but first efforts to mine such ore proved unprofitable. Later technological refinements would combine with amygdaloid finds to establish the area as one of the world's great mining centers.

Discovered a short time later was a third type of Copper Country deposit which would prove as much greater than the amygdaloids as the amygdaloids would to mass copper.

I am speaking of what miners commonly called "pudding stone" or conglomerate. The conglomerate beds were made up of sand, gravel and boulders left in depressions created by the advance and retreat of ice floes over the Copper Country during the glacial period. Copper was deposited with this pudding mixture and the whole thing was slowly cemented together with pure metal.[25]

The flint-hard pudding stone conglomerate — the copper being the pudding, would yield more dollars and copper per ton than even the richest amygdaloid beds, but advanced machinery would be needed to free conglomerate copper.

Mining companies were content to concentrate on exploiting the promising mass and amygdaloid deposits for the present.

The Quincy Mining Company, formed by members of the Isle Royale Mining

40

The Quincy site in winter.   Ron Avery

Company in 1852, was among the first to attempt mining operations on an amygdaloid lode. Early attempts near Houghton proved unsuccessful as the rock was simply too lean to work at a profit.[26] A few years later, 1856, the Pewabic Mining Company located a much richer lava bed nearby and subsequently combined with the Quincy Company to begin mining this new lode.

The ore body proved leaner than that in mass mines, but it was more regular and many times as extensive. The Quincy-Pewabic drifts (horizontal tunnels), eventually extended for thousands of feet. Shafts, often 20 feet wide, descended on a slight slant to 9,800 feet, almost a mile below sea level, without showing a marked decrease in yield.

Miners were also learning to accurately gauge the depth at which they could expect to find the copper bearing beds by calculating their predictable slant downward from the outer edge of the aforementioned stack of lava-copper saucers.

One story, related in nearly every book about Michigan copper mining, illustrates this accomplishment beautifully. This version appears in the *Arcadian Miner,* given to visitors at the underground Arcadian Mine attraction in Ripley.

"In August, 1895, when the Tamarack No. 5 mine near Calumet was started, mining captain William E. Parnell stated that the shaft would be bottomed in the lode at a depth of 4,650 feet, about January 1, 1902. The shaft actually cut the lode on December 20, 1901, at a depth of 4,662 feet, only 12 feet deeper and 11 days earlier than Parnell had predicted more than five years before."

The lode mentioned is the Calumet Conglomerate discovered later in the mining period, but the story indicates what was beginning to be done in the 1850's and 60's.

The ruins of hand-hewn farm buildings near Freda.
Hoyt Avery

Some of the guesswork was going out of Lake Superior copper mining as knowledge of the mineral belt increased. The belly laughs of oldtime mass miners subsided, became only occasional snickers and finally fell silent altogether. They slipped into bewildered but silent respect, as one "damn fool geologist" after another confidently pointed the way to copper fortunes. Mass mining was not the only way to mine copper. It simply took many years to prove the point to some. . . .[27]

Yet, as the mass mines grew barren and fell by the wayside, the one-time skeptics, now unemployed, found work aplenty in the booming amygdaloid mines of the region.

Not every new mining attempt brought wealth despite the growing geological knowledge illustrated above. Though the slope of the lava bed could be accurately predicted, there was always the possibility that nature had deposited only lava and gravel. There were some dismal failures.[28] The Keweenaw had a strange knack for keeping everyone honest, bestowing unbelievable wealth on some, making paupers of others!

In any event, the amygdaloid lodes were making — did make, the Copper Country into one of the really great mining districts of the world.

Hoisting machines of a magnitude never before dreamed of, were designed to lift hundreds of tons of Keweenaw rock from thousands of feet below the surface.

Great stamp mills were built to crush rock so metal seams and chunks could be separated from the poor rock before smelting.

All over the range the wilderness gave way to attractive communities housing miners, mill men and merchants. Settlers poured in from everywhere to work the mines, clear land and build farms and to establish businesses.

*Remains of the Gay Stamping Mill, built and operated
at Gay by the Mohawk Mining Company.* Hoyt Avery

If there was to become a synonym for amygdaloid mines, it would certainly be reliable or steady. The venerable Quincy, atop the hill overlooking Houghton and Hancock, produced more or less profitable amounts of copper from the Pewabic Lode for 50 years. It seemed to many that another unending storehouse of red metal had been discovered in the amygdaloid fields.

Other great deposits, most discovered prior to the Civil War, would prove nearly as rich as the Pewabic. The great Kearsarge Lode was mined for a continuous length of almost seven miles and yielded over $50 million in dividends. The famous Baltic Lode of the Copper Range Company was discovered in 1882, but didn't become an important producer until the turn of the century. The discovery paid $40 million in dividends during the first 15 years of intensive mining!

Immigration began turning the area into one of the world's great melting pots as Germans, Irish, Swedes, French, Finns, Italians and Cornish came pouring down the gangplank of every ship that landed in the Copper Country.

Thousands put everything they owned into a trip to the Lake Superior mining district. They fled the potato famine, European political upheavals and the declining mines of Cornwall. A million factors which had little or nothing to do with the Copper Country brought them here seeking economic salvation. They brought to Michigan not only their skill and youth, but a ready supply of high-class labor from the world's older mining and industrial centers.

With development of the Soo Locks in 1855, came increased immigration, commerce and cheaper copper shipping connections to eastern industrial markets. Railroads were soon serving the entire area. The Keweenaw was on its way to becoming a major industrial-mining-population center.

Overlooking the piles of poor rock and remaining build-ings at Central on the Keweenaw Peninsula. Several old buildings remain at this early mining site. Ron Avery

However, the United States stood on the verge of civil war when newly discovered amygdaloid deposits began coming into production. An uncertain economy caused the copper market to totter and then collapse during the first turbulent months of the War Between the States.

When copper fell to 17¢ a pound the mines ceased production, miners went payless and everyone waited anxiously to see what eastern industrialists and financiers would do next. Early Confederate victories added to the apprehension in the Copper Country, where more and more miners began looking to military service as the only way to make a living.

In 1862, however, the inertia seemed to transfer to the industrialized North and the Union Army. The copper market began an upward surge as the government sought metal for uniform brass, munitions, naval equipment and cannon.

The price leaped, again and again, upward to the unheard of level of nearly 50¢ a pound by 1864. Every mine in the district, even those earlier judged failures, began cashing in on the inflationary copper bonanza.

Every able-bodied man was pressed into service. Mining companies imported thousands of immigrants, either to work or to serve as substitute soldiers for those who would rather remain to mine copper. Marginally productive labor became a valuable commodity as producers attempted to replace enlistees — And mine output dropped!

Production finally stabilized due to increased employment, but the Copper Country was learning a bitter lesson in the economies of marginal production.

Miners sought high wages away from the deep-but-productive mines and they found companies, unable to turn a profit a few years earlier, more than willing to pay for their services now. The metallic contributions of these mines remained meager, but they were making a profit!

44

This same drama would be re-enacted during the First and Second World Wars although geologists knew by then that profitable reserves were nearing an end.

As the Civil War came to a close, copper prices once again slipped. Marginal operations could no longer compete and mines closed down all over the Peninsula. Beginning was a period of readjustment for the entire copper industry and it would require a period of years to reorganize, repair and rebuild.

The government had accumulated sizeable copper reserves which had to be disposed of. Thousands of tons of copper scrap were being recycled. The industrial sector needed time to regear itself to peacetime production markets...

This was a period of economic crisis — especially for investors — but a number of very significant wartime factors were already coming into play.

First, Michigan Lake Copper had so dominated the domestic market that the industry could adjust somewhat independently of declining world copper prices.

The great copper lodes had already been opened or were being opened at war's end. The tremendous expansion sparked by the wartime market did not end with Lee's surrender at Appomatox.

The conflict which left the South in ashes had left the Copper Country with only the prospect of even greater riches in amygdaloid and conglomerate copper, a vastly improved transportation and marketing network, a supply of modern mining tools and most importantly, the increased knowledge necessary to begin work on future bonanzas....

Many mines closed and many consolidated to avert financial disaster at war's end, but despite an aura of impending crisis, copper production quintupled between 1876 and 1884!

Old mining road near the Gratiot River, northeast of Mohawk.   Hoyt Avery

Dunes along Great Sand Bay near Jacob's Falls and Eagle Harbor. Thousands of visitors roam this wind-swept beach in search of plentiful Lake Superior agates.

Ron Avery

Remains of an old smoke stack at the No. 4 Kearsarge shaft near Copper City.

Hoyt Avery

Much of this is of course due to the rise of the Calumet and Hecla Mining Company which was a minor producer in 1866, but one which would account for 65 per cent of Copper Country output in 1872. The Calumet Conglomerate would prove to be one of the greatest treasure chests ever unearthed.[29]

Other companies were also increasing production. Air drills, improved blasting techniques, steam power, improved stamping and recovery methods, local smelting operations and a careful eye to automation and innovation drastically increased the production of the individual underground worker.[30]

All these factors would prove invaluable to the copper industry and America as they raced headlong together into the industrial age of electricity.

The Copper Country story from this point is one of incredible expansion and gradual decline as copper reserves ran out.

From the turn of the century until World War I, all stops would be pulled to meet the mushrooming domestic demand for copper. Consumption rose by one-third between 1898 and 1899. Electricity had become a fact of life! The Copper Country population soared correspondingly as prices remained relatively high and the market seemed insatiable. Completion of the Soo Canals and absence of immigration quotas made travel to the area a simple matter.

At the turn of the century, the copper district showed marked vitality as output continued to increase at about the same rate as other U.S. producers. Despite increased output, the Copper Country proportion of domestic production had fallen steadily from 51 per cent in 1886, to only 25 per cent in 1899. This was due to increased yields of the rapidly developing western copper mines which grabbed a sizeable portion of the expanding market.

The people of the copper district breathed easier, however, when their share of market production stabilized at approximately 25 per cent after 1900.

But ominous statistics, like those for the 1903 production year, were already beginning to whisper warnings of impending and certain doom in the violently competitive American metals market. To illustrate this fact with hard figures is to paint a picture of unmistakable meaning. For instance, Michigan companies raised 53 per cent of U.S. copper mining rock tonnage that year. They employed well over 50 per cent of the Nation's copper mining wage earners and approximately 70 per cent of the physical capital employed in the entire copper mining industry. All this machinery and manpower was employed to produce what had stabilized at 25 per cent of the domestic output of refined copper!

By 1900 the shafts of Keweenaw were the deepest in the world.[31] Bringing copper to the surface required increasing amounts of physical plant investment and it was apparent to geologists that the mines of the district had reached maturity.

Despite continued investments, greater depths would bring only a continued decline in copper content.

Rich deposits in Utah, Arizona, Nevada and Montana were producing ore containing from 3 to 5 per cent copper.

The Michigan conglomerate lodes had yielded as high as 4.5 per cent copper in 1883, but had slipped to less than 3 per cent by 1900. The old amygdaloids, yielding from 1.5 to 2 per cent copper in 1883, were producing only 1 per cent copper seven years later.

That the area was able to maintain its market percentage was primarily due to post-Civil War expansion of then newly located lodes.[32] They weren't nearly as rich or extensive as earlier discoveries, but their contribution greatly forestalled the region's decline.

Poor rock remaining at Minong Mine location, Isle Royale National Park. Ron Avery

Added to this was the declining, but still formidable influence of once dominant Copper Country producers within the market itself. They poured every available resource into mining efforts and organized an effective market structure which temporarily protected the region and would guarantee Lake copper's position for as long as possible.

Despite these stop-gaps, the end of an era was clearly in sight by 1900, but faith in the district overshadowed the good sense of most residents.

The mining boom in Michigan had already attained an unprecedented life-span and most were still certain of new ore discoveries which would maintain a competitive place for Michigan copper among world producers.

New finds of copper did keep coming to the surface, but the investment in new technology and prospecting was staggering.[33]

The period 1905-1918, is characterized by relatively high copper prices, an unprecedented increase in world copper consumption and the continual intro-duction of automated mining technology.

The battle to preserve Michigan's market status soon centered around efforts

Rock piles along Cliff Drive near site of Phoenix Mine.
Tom Avery

to keep production costs down. Longer hoists and underground rail systems were installed to move rock more quickly to the surface. Stamp mills had become much more efficient and a far greater percentage of copper was recovered from what would have been waste sand only a few years earlier.

New milling techniques made possible the low-cost reworking of 40 years of accumulated Calumet and Hecla tailings at a sizable profit.[34]

Labor costs remained low compared with those of Arizona and Montana producers, but so was per-man copper production which served to offset savings which might appear as great profit to investors.

Technology was making its greatest strides, enabling a single miner to produce many times the amount of ore he had in the past. Combined with selective mining methods, this per-man production factor grew dizzily and was a key factor in keeping the mines producing the same percentage of copper with reduced labor forces.

Michigan production continued to climb, going over 200 million pounds each year from 1905 to 1912, but the percentage of National production declined more or less steadily.

The huge production figures maintained the relative prosperity of the district. Dividends reached all time highs despite huge capital outlays.

The population rose to over 95,000 in 1910. New transportation systems linked mines with stamping mills and smelting operations. Attractive communities continued to flourish and expansion of cultural and business sectors was brisk.

Only the mines were wearing out!

*Hand-hewn log cabins which housed miners at Victoria,
near Rockland in the western portion of the mining
district.*   Hoyt Avery

There would be one more gigantic push for all out production during World War I and then the decline would begin to come more quickly.

Population was already beginning to drop by 1912. Automation was replacing manpower and miners left for employment elsewhere. Companies began selectively mining only the richest and most accessible rock.

The Copper Country story rotated around Calumet and Hecla operations which accounted for over 60 per cent of the district's production, but the rich conglomerate was not what it had once been.

Labor unrest was compounded by wartime manpower shortages. Wage increases could not reverse the first mass emigration from the copper district. Skilled labor drifted, then poured away to Detroit factories and other mining areas. It became obvious that the problems of the declining Superior copper industry would become even more acute in a postwar environment.

Between 1919 and 1938, the bottom would drop out of the Copper Country economy.

Calumet and Hecla expanded its output, but largely because many failing producers had been consolidated under its corporate wings.

In 1919, production fell to 180 million pounds from a wartime production high of nearly 270 million pounds. By 1921, output had fallen to about 90 million pounds, the lowest level for the district since 1889.

A brief period of postwar recovery came, reaching a peak in 1929. Then the Depression forced production below the 50 million pound mark in 1933. Output never again attained the average of the 1905-1912 production years. The end was in sight for any who would see it...

Lake Superior sunset at Hebard Park, just southwest of Copper Harbor.   Tom Avery

Population plummeted with lessening employment opportunities. As much as three-fifths of the population was on relief rolls during the Depression and one Hancock grocer was reportedly giving away shares of Calumet and Hecla stock with any $10 purchase!

Thousands who would have fled the district were stranded without money to travel or a place to go.

The federal government attempted mine relief operations, but it became apparent that the problem was not entirely the fault of the Depression. Even with huge subsidies, the mining of Lake copper was only marginally profitable. Mining became still more selective and production per underground employee increased measurably, but failure was inevitable. . . .

By 1940, population had declined to the level of 1890 and employment in the mines had slipped below the level of 1870!

The population declined further during World War II and those who remained found employment scarce when hostilities had ended and production subsidies were lifted.

The mild recession of 1949 again put more than a third of the work force in unemployment lines. The population declined even more rapidly and it became evident that the outflow was not to be reversed by new discoveries of copper.

Labor disputes during the 1950's and 1960's compounded problems. Copper markets, dependent on the availability of other ores, often suffered one reverse after another as strikes curtailed coal, steel and various production industries.

Workers everywhere bargained for higher wages, but the remaining Copper

*Douglas Houghton Falls between Laurium and Lake
Linden.*   Hoyt Avery

Country producers felt the pinch more than most. They negotiated, pointed to
exhausted resources and dwindling returns on investments. The mines began
to close and they closed with what seemed like certain finality. Smelting and
tailing recovery operations would go on for sometime, but the Michigan
copper boom had ended.

Remains of an old engine house at Baltic location.

Hoyt Avery

The Presque Isle River along the western boundry of the Porcupine Mountains State Park.   Hoyt Avery

Sunrise at Moskey Basin, Isle Royale National Park.
Ron Avery

THOUGHTS ON WHAT REMAINS

A thousand varied impressions register in the mind of the professional photographer as he compiles material for a book on the Michigan Copper Country. His success or failure depends largely on his ability to recognize and record those things which others might overlook, those things which are enough out of the ordinary to capture interest and those things which best tell the story of the country where he works —

The Copper Country presents vast and challenging subject matter. A beautiful and majestic Lake Superior shoreline, windswept mountains, wildlife, dense woodlands and virgin forests, splendid rivers, remote waterfalls, Isle Royale — absolutely breathtaking scenery abounds.

The area remains rugged, largely untrammeled and in constant change. To best capture the moods of the region requires that it be seen in the brilliant sunshine of summer, the vivid color, driving rains and dense fogs of autumn, the deep snows of winter and the roar of the spring breakup.

Every hour of every season sheds a different light and changing mood on the landscape.

To cuss the wind and fog atop Brockway Mountain Drive on one day is to more appreciate the clear skies and the eagle's view at the Lake of the Clouds the next. And all the while those thousand impressions are falling into place....

It takes time, much more than the average visitor has, to really capture a feeling for this country. Nearly a year's work, with three of us toting cameras, went into creating this volume. Years of training and working together came earlier, but our pictures reflect those things which struck each of us as unique, important or representative of the story we individually sensed and had attempted to relate.

We sometimes disagreed as to which picture best portrays a particular thought or captures a fleeting mood. This is certainly not uncommon, but interestingly, a single observation pervaded our collective notes on the Copper Country.

One impression overshadowed and served to form all others — again and again, each of us noted the stoic permanence radiated by the entire region.

Old pine at Porcupine Mountains State Park near Ontonagon.   Hoyt Avery

Huge stone dinosaurs overlook Brockway Mountain Drive Creek and the surrounding countryside from near the top of the mountain. Tom Avery

Autumn along Brockway Mountain Drive near Copper Harbor. No Copper Country visitor should miss this beautiful drive. Hoyt Avery

The millions of dollars spent to remove billions of tons of rock and copper have left relatively minor scars on the mining district. The scenery of the Lake Superior Copper Country remains so spectacular that, as mentioned in the introduction, one must continually remind himself that the area became famous for copper mining!

The 120 years of the copper boom constituted only a fraction of a second in the life of the landscape. Here again our notes reflected similar thoughts, to the effect that the copper boom both began and began to end with removal of the first piece of metal from the region. Every pound of copper removed lessened the amount which remained by one pound. . . .

Measured in terms of human expenditure and reward the copper boom had great local and national significance, but already the elements and the country itself have reduced much of the evidence of inroads once made by modern man.

Each year takes an increasing toll on the trappings of early settlement. Every passing season changes the country to resemble more closely what must have existed when the first men came here for copper thousands of years ago.

This feeling is overwhelming as one backpacks the near wilderness of Isle Royale National Park. All evidence of modern mining has been removed or left to deteriorate before the elements.

A visit to Isle Royale takes one as close to what wilderness is, as he is likely to ever come. To fly over the islands offers one a glimpse of a wilderness where the balance of nature remains relatively undisturbed. . . . One's thoughts are certainly mixed as he races above the islands and Lake Superior to keep an appointment on the mainland!

In any case, a visit to the islands also provides the observer with an example by which to gauge the deterioration of modern man's artifacts. The process is well under way throughout the district.

On the mainland, modern highways carry thousands of tourists to Keweenaw, Houghton and Ontonagon Counties to see where copper had been mined — and yet it is the outstanding scenery which they invariably recall!

Many visitors comment on the sense of inspiration or exhilaration they experience from simply traveling through an area still touched by wilderness. Most seem far more impressed by the agate beaches of majestic Lake Superior than by the pioneer accomplishments which first opened the area. For a majority of tourists, man's handiwork serves to set off the scenery, making it even more spectacular by comparison.

The photographer certainly shares some of these feelings, but his year-round presence in the region tempers his observations with a growing appreciation for what man has left of himself, what those things relate about his life here — and what the form of a tumbling building, a line of trees or a crumbling foundation does to enhance the scenery. . . .

It may be an unfair comment on 20th Century life, but the trappings of 100 years ago seem much more at home in this ageless landscape than the yellow and black signs at every curve, the rows of utility poles which parallel highways, or the various no trespassing and real estate signs. Even the winding roadways seem out of place on occasion.

Old things seem to belong here as part of the country. Even though they came in the same manner as the more modern additions just mentioned, they seem to offer more intense, more meaningful comment on the history of the

Beaver ponds near Minong Mine on Isle Royale National Park.   Ron Avery

Young bull moose near Mud Lake, Isle Royale National Park.   Martin Grosnick

Decaying evidence of man's efforts to mine copper at
Phoenix.   Tom Avery

area. As one spends extended time here he becomes aware of more and more such signposts from the past. Each remnant relates a sentence or two which has relevance to the romantic history of the region. Together they blend into a running commentary on the life and times of the Copper Country; its culture, people, environment — all related in a story with picture puzzle parts. . . .

For example, the cemeteries date to earliest days of the district and ironically say much about life during the boom days. Life expectancy was short. Infant mortality was very high and fever, pneumonia and childbirth were major causes of death.

Stones usually carry birth and death dates, causes of death, home of origin and sometimes religious convictions.

Many died in mining accidents and many had come here from Cornwall, Ireland and Germany.

A comment on environment, primitive housing and nonexistent medical facilities is etched here in stone. . . . To be born during a Copper Country fall or winter was often a fatal mistake in timing!

Such is the commentary I speak of. . . . Although few single discoveries relate so much information.

Some signposts are little more than regional idiosyncrasies, like the uncommonly tall fire hydrants found in some communities. They, like the elevated porches and doorways of many homes, are alterations made necessary by extremely heavy snowfalls.

Building design often indicates much about the people who settled here. The hand-hewn log homes were usually constructed by Scandinavian immigrants. These early structures were built of solid logs, squared with a broadaxe

Hoar frost covering shore growth along the Gratiot River north of Ahmeek.   Ron Avery

and dovetailed together at the corners. A few such homes remain in the earliest mining areas.

The neat rows of nearly identical, two-story frame buildings which appear in other areas came much later. These generally represented company towns, constructed to house as many workers as possible at a point near one of the larger mining operations. Most such communities have lapsed into disrepair, but some were well maintained and still house year 'round residents.

The daughter of one immigrant miner recalled the company home offered to her father during the depression at a cash price of $25. She explained how he had to refuse because he didn't have enough money!

Rows of neatly spaced Lombardy Poplars are evident along a number of Copper Country hillsides. Native to Europe, the trees were probably brought here as reminders of far distant homelands.

Also evident around nearly every mining location are scraggly little apple trees. Apples are one of the few fruits which would ripen during the short Upper Peninsula growing season. They seem to stand as sentinels wherever

Mining road near Rockland and old Victoria Mine location.
                                                    Hoyt Avery

settlement took place. In many places they are all that remains of what may have been a pioneer homestead. One can only theorize as to what happened to the buildings which must have stood nearby.

Beautifully ornate opera houses were the cultural centers of the large Copper Country communities.[35] Now closed or serving as movie theaters, they once featured entertainment on a par with anything available in the east.

The design of opera houses, churches and municipal buildings often reflects strong ties with New England the attempts to transplant a familiar social and cultural heritage in the remote Copper Country.

Along the shores of both sides of the Peninsula, deserted boathouses and rotting nets tell something of a once thriving fishing industry. Old fishing boats rest nearby — some atop skids and others just dumped on shore. All are in disrepair, victims of a declining population and years of rugged use.

Many lighthouses once ringed the Keweenaw shoreline and Isle Royale. Many are gone, some are boarded up, others have been purchased and remain in varied stages of deterioration or restoration and some still guide shipping around the rugged coast.

Company houses standing empty at Painsdale, south of Houghton on M-26.   Hoyt Avery

All tell of days when ships hauled load after load of miners, cargo, and copper upon the treacherous lake. To visualize this area without modern highways is to realize the importance of Great Lakes transportation. Settlements sprang up near safe ports. Exploration, early mining development, construction of inland transportation routes were begun at, and largely dictated by, the sites of shipping facilities.

Everything came and went by water during the early days of the Copper Country. A great many vessels were lost on the lake or torn apart along the rocky coastline. Many lives were lost in efforts to supply the early mining camps. Anyone who has ever been in the Copper Country during a November gale can imagine the apprehension of an isolated mining community as it awaited provisions or transport on the final ship of the season. Modern lake freighters still lose an occasional battle with Lake Superior. It seems incredible that the ships of 100 years ago could have withstood a raging lake storm!

The remains of other man-made objects make it possible for visitors to trace the route of copper from mine to market with very little knowledge of the actual processes involved.

Old railbeds, overgrown and deserted, often run near rusting shaft houses. The copper bearing rock was hauled in wooden ore cars from here to a stamp mill where huge machines pulverized it.

A tremendous amount of water was required to remove the metal from the worthless sand and some sort of water impoundment still exists near many of the area's mines. Huge wooden and earth-filled dams like those near Red Ridge and Victoria and in the hills above Central are excellent illustrations.

Mountains of stamp sand, disposed of near Lake Linden and to lesser extents

Old fishing tug near Ontonagon.   Hoyt Avery

throughout the area, are evidence of the operations which went on at the various mining locations.

Slag, created when copper was smelted, is visible at several points near Houghton and Hancock. Here 99 per cent pure copper was readied for shipment to market.

Probably the most difficult areas to locate are the actual sites of the old mine shafts themselves. Nearly all of them have been filled to prevent accidents and they are lost amid the poor rock and rubble of the general area where they descended. In winter, however, many old shafts are easily pinpointed as the warm, damp air below the surface rises and forms clouds of steam in the frigid air above.

There are hundreds of simple observations which could be drawn from the remains of the mining sites.

That some modern shaft houses remain, are maintained and lighted at night, is evidence of continued faith in the reopening of the district.

The nature of the country itself has had much to say about how and where development took place. Obviously, the existence of copper and access to transportation facilities were major considerations, but the presence of dense forests or raging streams sometimes dictated community location.

To see the Sturgeon, Presque Isle, Ontonagon or Eagle Rivers during the spring thaw is to see unimaginable water power resources. Communities grew as close to such streams as possible.

Even the presence of wildlife provides commentary on the history and romance of the Copper Country.

The intricate mazes of beaver dams and ponds, especially fascinating on Isle Royale, bring to mind the men who first explored this region. They came to

Overlooking Lake Superior shipping routes from Shore-line Drive near Agate Harbor. Hoyt Avery

*Overlooking the Victoria Dam and Backwater on the
Ontonagon River.* Hoyt Avery

*The roaring Presque Isle Falls, near the western edge
of Porcupine Mountains State Park.* Hoyt Avery

Aging beaver cuttings, Isle Royale National Park.

Ron Avery

harvest furs. Their stories of copper added great momentum to development and exploration. Ultimately responsible for copper discoveries were the unassuming beaver — building dams, felling trees and supplying hats for eastern and European gentlemen.

The list of interesting observations which might be made is endless — Certainly all this geo-history is interrelated and spurs further thought as to what happened, where, how and why....

One can halt these mind games at any point in his discovery of the Copper Country, but a single observation transcends all others and puts them in perspective.

It is impossible to visit this rugged mining district, to view its jagged beaches, the mountains which back them up, the rivers, streams and islands of the Copper Country without falling in love with the stark beauty of the landscape.

Sunset at Esrey Park near Eagle Harbor.   Hoyt Avery

The area is splendid, inspiring and sometimes cruel. Here is a country to be lived with, endured, admired, but never tamed or greatly altered by the presence of mere man.

If everyone left the Copper Country today and the area remained unentered for the next 1,000 years — I'd venture that first explorers would find a wilderness, unbroken except for the ancient copper mines of some absent civilization.

ABOUT THE PHOTOGRAPHERS

The Averys; Hoyt, Ron and Tom, have spent their lives in a world of shutter speeds, lenses, developers, exposure meters and printing presses.

HOYT, a nature lover, artist with a camera and a self-taught printer, has long been a master of scenic photography. His work is deliberate and concise, adding balance to the work of his sons. Each of his pictures becomes an expression of perfection and eye-retaining composition. Nothing bothers him more than the sign that breaks the lines of an otherwise beautiful landscape. His type of picture becomes more difficult to find each day.

RON, the youngest of the Avery trio, is an outdoorsman who sees pictures in almost everything. His ability to deliberately compose a striking picture is evident in this volume, but his favorites are always the simple masterpieces of snakes, frogs, weeds — that most people walk by without even seeing. He was in his glory on Isle Royale where that type of subject matter was everywhere. He'll certainly be ready to tackle the project that will enable us to use more of such interesting material.

Also deserving mention is the senior member of the Avery photographic family, NORTON AVERY, who spent his "vacation" snooping around for material in the Copper Country. Rain and dense fog proved a problem in the week devoted to *Copper Country — God's Country*, but a few seconds of sunlight were all he needed to capture the sparkling stream at the old Cliff Mine location.

A comment is also warranted here about a young Copper Country photographer who helped us out with the moose picture in this volume. **MARTIN GROSNICK,** who worked as postmaster on Isle Royale National Park, captured this fellow on film several years ago. This is the first time we've ever incorporated a photograph by a non-Avery in our work, but this was an outstanding picture which said much about the wilderness nature of Isle Royale.

AND THE AUTHOR

TOM, the reflective writer-photographer of this volume, views pictures as they relate to the story in his notes. He was recording impressions on the Copper Country from Isle Royale to Ontonagon. The observations formed mental pictures which he sought to locate and capture on film. He feels that enough pictures of the little things in any given area can tell more about life there than any number of words — And still there are always things which one will overlook or fail to interpret correctly. Even when a picture portrays ten thousand words, there is always a line of comment which can make a picture say more. His idea of a great picture or story is one that makes the reader ask the same questions he asked when he took it or scribbled it down.

FOR THE SHUTTERBUG

The reproductions in this volume are all from 35mm or 2¼ x 3¼ AGFA-CHROME transparencies. Our equipment consisted of two converted 4 x 5 Linhof Technikas, two 35mm Exaktas and a 35mm Pentax. All exposure readings were taken with external meters and the only filter ever employed was a polarizing filter.

Our studios at AuTrain are always open to anyone who wishes to see our equipment and print shop. The welcome mat is always out for the traveler interested in talking photography and we're always happy to help in whatever way we can to make travels in the Upper Peninsula more enjoyable.

AUTHOR'S NOTES

1. Some historians discount the story of Franklin's role in Copper Country history. Accounts have no doubt been romanticized by the local citizenry, but I find it impossible to ignore either the strange international boundary line in Lake Superior or specific references to non-existent Isle Philippeaux in the Treaty of Paris, 1783.
2. The first account of the Michigan Copper Country was published by Lagarde in Paris, 1636.
3. Pierre Boucher, a Paris publisher and traveler, compiled the first widely read volume of reports on the Copper region in 1640.
4. The Jesuit Relations were published as reports of French missionary and exploration efforts from 1636. These often exaggerated but well read reports, did much to stir French interest in the New World and insured a continual flow of money to support further discovery and missionary efforts among the Indians. This particular observation was recorded by a Jesuit father in the Relations de ce qui s'est passe dens le pays des Hurons, 1655-60.
5. Nonexistent Isle Philippeaux (the spelling varies), is the only Lake Superior island specifically mentioned in the geographic boundaries section of the Treaty of Paris, 1783.
6. The Northwest Ordinance, 1787, established territories, defined requirements for statehood, outlined governmental organization, etc., and effectively hastened the settlement of western frontier lands. It also acted to lessen the importance of any New World claims still maintained by European powers.
7. Some historians maintain that the Indians kept the location of ancient mines a well guarded secret. Explorers and archeologists contend that the natives would have revealed the locations had they known them.
8. Though the Indians knew of the hammerstones, they knew very little of copper mining. The copper and stone tools employed by Michigan Indians when first encountered by European explorers, were less sophisticated than those used by the ancient miners 3,500 years earlier. Many hammered copper knives, arrow and spear heads and axes were recovered at ancient mining sites. Some fine examples are on display at Fort Wilkins and Rockland Historical Society museums.
9. All but two modern mines were put down on locations where prehistoric mines are known to have been worked.
10. A similar method was employed at some Copper Country mines until sophisticated stamping operations were developed in the 1860's.
11. Between 1929 and 1949, the Calumet and Hecla Company mined 509 million pounds of copper with practically all energy from electric power.
12. Pure native copper was discovered in Bolivia in 1925. Until then, Keweenaw copper was viewed as a freak of nature and something many old miners wouldn't believe, even after they'd seen it!
13. In 1834, the Michigan Territory included the Upper and Lower Peninsulas, nearly all of Wisconsin and a large part of what is now Minnesota.
14. The Ontonagon Boulder is now on display in the Smithsonian Institution, established in Washington, D.C., 1846.
15. Houghton, a popular wit and lecturer in Detroit social circles, left a thriving medical practice to explore the Keweenaw region. The New York native was killed when his boat swamped near Eagle River in 1845. A modest monument stands at Eagle River and the principal city of the area bears his name.

16. The $3,000 designated by the State Legislature financed exploration of an area which would pay over $350 million in mining dividends alone by 1960.

17. This interesting journal was published by the John M. Longyear Research Library, Marquette, Michigan in 1970. Many of the place names are not accurate, however, and understanding requires a fair amount of familiarity with the region . . . and a very complete map.

18. Miners scoffed at anything other than mass copper, but even the Isle Royale operation paid more in dividends than all but a few of the "great" mass mines.

19. The mass mine "bonanzas" (like the Cliff and Minesota), were the yardsticks by which early mines were measured. Prospectors sneered at attempts to work the amygdaloid and conglomerate lodes although the success ratio and dividend payments, dwarfed those of mass mining efforts which collectively lost far more money than they made. For example, of the 112 mining corporations which operated in Ontonagon County, only the Minesota paid more in dividends than it collected in assessments — Paid a profit!

20. The Boston and Pittsburgh areas were early centers of the American metal industry. To find copper in Michigan was to assure an expanding and more diversified industry. It is interesting to note that many of the companies which discontinued mining operations in the Upper Peninsula, remain among the leaders in American metallurgy.

21. The discovery of the Cliff deposit is credited to so many individuals that I've not expounded on any of them, lest I confuse the issue further. I have treated the discovery of the Calumet Conglomerate in the same manner although it appears that Edwin Hulbert indeed, made this discovery. The stories surrounding both finds are extremely interesting and I urge the serious history buff to dig into the varied reports of the day.

22. This figure reflects the cost of closing down operations at Copper Harbor and beginning work on the Cliff location.

23. Despite all the fuss over the great mass mines, the chunks of pure metal taken from them accounts for less than 3 per cent of the copper produced in the district between 1845 and 1950.

24. The curve of the lava beds is attributed to geologic upheavals which came long after the area was created. A sort of settling process caused the entire country to tilt on its side along a predictable 56 degree angle. When geologists had learned this, much of the guesswork went out of predicting the depths at which the copper bearing rock would be encountered.

25. The conglomerate locations were the only areas left unworked by prehistoric miners. A storage pit containing hammering stones and mass copper was discovered near the Calumet Conglomerate, but no evidence of actual mining existed.

26. Amygdaloid ores contained from 2 to 5 per cent copper. What looked like a very lean deposit could probably have been worked at a comfortable profit, had more sophisticated recovery techniques been available. Even on profitable lodes, a tremendous amount of copper went out with the stamp sands and was discarded as waste.

27. It is interesting to read the comments of early miners with respect to amygdaloid and conglomerate copper. The fact that mines had been discovered without geologists seemed reason enough to disregard what they had to say about the potential of a particular site!

28. Notable among failures is the Arcadian Copper Company formed in 1899. The company purchased 4,000 acres, built 150 homes, constructed stamp mills, surface buildings and a business section, employed nearly 2,000 workers and mining was begun. . . . In 1904, you could have purchased stock in a company, which had spent well over $2 million on development, for 25¢ per share. There simply wasn't any copper at the bottom of the splendid shafts!

29. Two companies alone, Calumet and Hecla (mining the Calumet Conglomerate), and Quincy (mining the Pewabic Amgydaloid Lode), have paid far more than all the moneys spent on all the mining ventures ever attempted in Michigan. Until recent times, Calumet and Hecla eclipsed any mine in the world, irrespective of metal or product mined, in dollar value of the ores extracted from the earth.

30. The district as a whole was producing approximately 12,000 pounds of copper per man-year of labor in 1909. This figure doubled by 1929, despite lower copper content of the rock being worked.

31. The deepest shaft in North America, Quincy, descends on a slight angle to 9,800 feet, approximately a mile below sea level. Four-fifths of its depth is below the level of nearby Portage Lake.

32. The Calumet Conglomerate, the Baltic, Champion, Kearsarge, Ahmeek and Allouez mines were among those properties which filled the gap left by declining production in the district's older mines. To say that they were not as rich may be misleading, for the Calumet Conglomerate was certainly on a par with the nation's greatest mine, but the output was dwindling in comparison to developing western properties.

33. The Michigan Copper Country became an experimental laboratory for dozens of mining developments. The companies were anxious for any inventions which would allow them to maintain market status, increase per man production or lower labor costs.

34. After the Depression, during World War II and for several years after, recovery of copper from these tailings would be the major source of the district's percentage of the national output. To gain an idea of how much stamp sand was available, consider that Portage Lake, more than 1,200 feet wide at Ripley in 1860, was narrowed by more than half by stamp sands dumped from mills on both sides of the canal!

35. The theater enjoyed great popularity in the Copper Country around the turn of the century. In the 1890's Houghton had two theaters, as did Hancock, while Lake Linden, Calumet, and Laurium each had its own opera house or theater. In 1898, Laurium built an opera house to seat 1,300 people. The people of Calumet quickly spent $73,000 for an elaborately decorated theater which opened in 1900, to an audience of over 1,200. The Kerredge Theater, opened in Hancock in 1902, had a seating capacity of 1,565, a stage 40 feet deep and 70 feet wide, 10 dressing rooms and a thousand electric lamps. Box seats for the opening performance went at $40. A sellout crowd jammed the theater!

Bibliography

BOOKS

Ashley, Ossian D. *The Copper Mines of Lake Superior.* Hyde Park, Mass.: Norfolk County Gazette Press, 1873.

Bailey, Thomas A. *A Diplomatic History of The American People.* New York, Meredith Publishing Company, 1968.

Bebeau, Joseph. *A Story Of Early Days In Rockland, Michigan.* Rockland, Centennial Committee, 1947.

Benedict, Harry C. *Red Metal: The Calumet and Hecla Story.* Ann Arbor, University of Michigan Press, 1951.

Bening, Arthur C. and Thomas C. Cochran. *The Rise of American Economic Life.* New York, Charles Scribner's Sons, 1964.

Carter, James L. and Ernest H. Rankin, ed. *North to Lake Superior; The Journal of Charles W. Penny, 1840.* Marquette, Michigan, The John M. Longyear Research Library, 1970.

Chaput, Donald. *The Cliff; America's First Great Copper Mine.* Kalamazoo, Michigan, Sequoia Press, 1971.

Drier and DuTemple — Professor Roy W. Drier and Octave J. DuTemple. *Prehistoric Copper Mining in the Lake Superior Region.* Calumet, Michigan, Published privately, 1961.

Dunbar, Willis F. *Michigan: A History of the Wolverine State.* Grand Rapids, William B. Eerdmans Publishing, 1965.

Gates, William B. Jr. *Michigan Copper and Boston Dollars: An Economic History of the Michigan Copper Mining Industry.* Massachusetts, Harvard University Press, 1951.

Glasscock, Carl B. *The War of the Copper Kings.* Indianapolis, Bobbs-Merrill Company, 1935.

Jamison, James K. *This Ontonagon County.* Ontonagon, The Ontonagon Herald Company, 1939.

Joralemon, Ira B. *Romantic Copper — Its Lure and Lore.* New York, D. Appleton Century Company, 1936.

Michigan: A Guide to the Wolverine State. A Michigan Writers' Project, New York, Oxford University Press, 1941.

Murdoch, William Angus. *Boom Copper: The Story of the First United States Mining Boom.* New York, Macmillan Company, 1943.

Rickard, T. A. *The Copper Mines of Lake Superior.* New York, The Engineering and Mining Journal, 1905.

Robinson, Orrin W. *Early Days of the Lake Superior Copper Country.* Houghton by D. C. Robinson, 1938.

Wexler, Imanuel. *Fundamentals of International Economics.* New York, Random House, 1969.

Information was also gathered from United States census statistics, numerous newspaper articles and brief reports of local historical groups. Also helpful were the publications of the United States Department of the Interior, National Park Service, Government Printing Office, Washington, D.C.

ACKNOWLEDGMENTS

Many people have made this book possible. . . .

We wish to express our appreciation to all of them and especially to Mr. and Mrs. Donald Doyle of Copper Harbor, Mr. and Mrs. Dennis Ross of Ontonagon and Mr. and Mrs. Donald Koop of Eagle Harbor. They were the ones who were ready to wholeheartedly back our efforts when *Copper Country — God's Country* was still in the idea stage. Their faith in our creative ability has been most gratifying.

We also received encouragement and invaluable assistance from Mr. and Mrs. Ike Lundberg at Fort Wilkins State Park, Mr. Louis Keopel of the Quincy Mining Company at Ripley, and Mr. Hugh Beattie, Superintendent of Isle Royale National Park.

If you enjoy this volume, we hope you'll tell some of these Copper Country residents about it. . . . Without them it couldn't have been done!

We also thank Mr. Steve Wright, now teaching at UCLA, for his careful editing of a half-scribbled manuscript.

ALSO AVAILABLE from Avery Color Studios, "SLOW ME DOWN, LORD!"

A Pictorial Study of Wilderness . . . set in the recently created Pictured Rocks National Lakeshore, the photographs and text in this work are aimed at making every reader more aware of the intricate natural relationships and beauties which surround us everywhere. Exploring a relatively small geographic area, "SLOW ME DOWN, LORD!" is designed to make people see and appreciate a world they may have walked past or crushed under foot before.